Way to Be!

Manners in Public

by **Carrie Finn**   illustrated by **Chris Lensch**

PICTURE WINDOW BOOKS
Minneapolis, Minnesota

Special thanks to our advisers for their expertise:

Kay Augustine, Associate Director
Institute for Character Development at Drake University

Susan Kesselring, M.A., Literacy Educator
Rosemount–Apple Valley–Eagan (Minnesota) School District

Editor: Nick Healy
Designer: Tracy Davies
Page Production: Brandie Shoemaker
Art Director: Nathan Gassman
Associate Managing Editor: Christianne Jones
The illustrations in this book were created digitally.

Picture Window Books
151 Good Counsel Drive
P.O. Box 669
Mankato, MN 56002-0669
877-845-8392
www.picturewindowbooks.com

Printed in China.

Library of Congress Cataloging-in-Publication Data
Finn, Carrie.
Manners in public / by Carrie Finn ; illustrated by
Chris Lensch.
p. cm. – (Way to be!)
Includes bibliographical references and index.
ISBN-13: 978-1-4048-3153-7 (library binding)
ISBN-13: 978-1-4048-3555-9 (paperback)
ISBN-13: 978-1-4048-5993-7 (paperback)
1. Etiquette for children and teenagers–Juvenile
literature. I. Lensch, Chris. II. Title.
BJ1857.C5F48 2007
395.5'3–dc22   2006027301

Whether you are at the park, the movies, or the store, you can use good manners. In fact, good manners come in handy anytime you are out and about.

There are lots of ways you can use good manners in public.

Calvin says "Good morning, Mr. Jeffers!" when he gets on the school bus.

He says "Have a good night, Mr. Jeffers. Thank you!" when he gets off the bus at the end of the day.

He is using good manners.

Erik goes to the pet store to look at fish. He says "Excuse me" when he bumps into someone.

He is using good manners.

When Dawn finds a toy elephant on the sidewalk, she takes it back to her neighbors' house.

She is using good manners.

Jude uses the sidewalk on his way home from school. He stays out of people's yards.

He is using good manners.

Clara and Mitchell throw their trash in the bin after their picnic in the park.

They are using good manners.

Annika says "Thank you" when the waiter brings her hamburger.

She is using good manners.

Jack loves space movies. Still, he goes to the back of the ticket line at the theater. He waits his turn.

He is using good manners.

Lorna does not shout when she spots her friend Chloe at the museum. She walks over to Chloe and says hello.

She is using good manners.

At the market, June asks, "Mom, may I please have a treat?" If her mom says no, June does not argue.

She is using good manners.

It's easy to use good manners in your neighborhood, at the store, or in a restaurant. When you do, you will find that people treat you kindly in return.

Fun Facts

In China, people with good manners do not point when speaking.

In Venezuela, people with good manners sit up straight. Poor posture is thought to be rude.

In Peru, it is polite to rest both hands on the table when eating out.

Japanese people bow to greet one another.

In Saudi Arabia, it is thought to be rude to eat with the left hand.

In South Korea, people with good manners do not blow their nose at the table.

To Learn More

At the Library

Candell, Arianna. *Mind Your Manners: At Parties.* Hauppauge, N.Y.: Barron's, 2005.

DeGezelle, Terri. *Manners at a Restaurant.* Mankato, Minn.: Capstone Press, 2005.

Willems, Mo. *Time to Say Please!* New York: Hyperion, 2005.

On the Web

FactHound offers a safe, fun way to find Web sites related to this book.
All of the sites on FactHound have been researched by our staff.

1. Visit *www.facthound.com*
2. Type in this special code: 1404831533
3. Click on the FETCH IT button.

Your trusty FactHound will fetch the best sites for you!

Index

Look for all of the books in the Way to Be! series:

Being a Good Citizen: A Book About Citizenship

Being Fair: A Book About Fairness

Being Respectful: A Book About Respectfulness

Being Responsible: A Book About Responsibility

Being Trustworthy: A Book About Trustworthiness

Caring: A Book About Caring

Manners at School

Manners at the Table

Manners in Public

Manners in the Library

Manners on the Playground

Manners on the Telephone